20:45: Unlocking Your Inner Magic

A Practical Handbook for Teen Self-Awareness

STASIA SMITH

DEDICATION

I dedicate this book to the incredible teenagers across the world embarking on a journey of self-discovery. May these pages be your guiding light as you uncover the extraordinary uniqueness within each of you. Embrace your individuality, for it is the source of your boundless potential.

CONTENTS

INTRODUCTION

Dear Reader,

Welcome to an incredible journey within yourself. This book is your key to unlocking the magic that resides in you. No matter your age the power of self-discovery, growth, and making life choices that truly matter.

This magic isn't about wizards or spells; it's about understanding yourself, managing your emotions, and listening to your inner voice. It's about finding your path and making heart-based decisions.

You have two paths to choose from:

1. Read and practice at your own pace.
2. Read slowly, practice as you go, and savor each lesson in your own time. Your journey, your speed.

Remember, it's okay not to have all the answers now. Keep exploring, learning, and listening to your heart. Your soul is your reliable guide, leading you to a future filled with joy and fulfillment.

By the way, I've set aside a special section at the end of this book for you. It's your personal journal to jot down your thoughts and reflections, especially after trying out the cool practices I shared. Make this book uniquely yours by using it to capture your ideas as you read!

Are you ready for this exciting journey of self-discovery? The magic is within you. Let's begin!

Warmly,
Stasia

CHAPTER 1

THE IMPORTANCE OF SELF-LOVE

In a world filled with endless adventures and mysteries waiting to be explored, there is something truly special that we must always remember. It's a simple yet powerful idea that can make a world of difference in our lives. So, let's embark on this journey of self-discovery and learn the art of self-love.

Imagine yourself standing on the edge of a vast ocean, gazing at the horizon where the sky kisses the sea. This ocean represents your life, and within it lies the treasure of self-love. Now, you might be thinking, "What's so important about self-love?"

Well, my dear friend, it's not about being selfish or thinking only about yourself. It's about something much more beautiful. It's about what you are, it's about who you are. It's about opening your heart, just like you do when you love your family, your friends, or even your beloved pet. Think about that person or pet you love so deeply that you can't help but smile when you see them. That feeling, that warmth in your heart—that's love.

Now, here's the secret: that same love you give to others should also be given to yourself. Yes, you are just as important as the people and pets you hold dear. In fact, you are the most significant person in your own Universe.

Sometimes, people might say, "You think only about yourself, you're selfish." But remember, they might not fully understand the difference between selfishness and self-love. Selfishness is when you care only about yourself, without any consideration for others. Self-love, on the other hand, is like a warm hug for your own heart. It means caring for yourself in a way that makes you a happier, kinder, and more loving person to everyone around you.

So, my young adventurer, as you embark on this journey through the pages of this book, keep in mind the importance of self-love. Just like you care for the people and things you cherish, remember to treat yourself with kindness and affection. When you do, you'll discover a well of love within your heart that can make your life truly extraordinary.

Practice:

Let's begin our journey of self-love with a simple practice.

1. Find a quiet and comfortable place where you won't be disturbed. You can even play some soft and relaxing music to create a peaceful atmosphere.

2. Sit up straight with your hands resting on your knees, palms facing up. Alternatively, you can lie down without a pillow and stretch your arms out like a star.

3. Now, close your eyes and take a deep breath. Feel the air filling your lungs and then slowly exhale. As you exhale, imagine that each breath is flowing out through your heart, as if you're exhaling through the centre of your chest.

4. With each breath out, let a warm and comforting sensation fill your heart. It's like a gentle, loving energy radiating from that special place in your chest. Keep focusing on your breath, and as you continue to exhale through

your heart, say to yourself, "I am." Feel those words resonate within you.

5. Repeat this practice for about 5 minutes. As you do, visualize the warmth and love spreading from your heart throughout your entire body. Feel the love and kindness you're giving to yourself. Remember, it's not selfish, it's self-love.

You can do this practice anytime and for as long as you'd like. However, what's more important than the duration is consistency. Try to make it a part of your daily routine. You can do it in the morning right after waking up to start your day with self-love, or you can practice it before falling asleep to unwind and relax. You can even do it during the daytime whenever you have a few moments of free time.

Before we dive into how to use this practice when things get wild during the day, remember this: You're a one-of-a-kind, amazing individual in this vast Universe, and guess what? You totally deserve love – starting with the love you give yourself. Take a few moments daily to connect with your heart and appreciate your awesomeness. It's like watering your inner self-love garden, and the cool thing is, when you show love to yourself, the Universe often sends extra love your way.

But now, let's chat about what to do on those crazy days when life's on fast-forward and you're just rolling with it. We've got a nifty trick for you to quickly reconnect with yourself, even in just 1-2 minutes.

Quick Me-Time Break:

1. Mini Chill Time: Find a quiet moment, even if it's just a breather between classes or while waiting for a text reply.

2. Stay Earthed: Start by tuning into your feet. Maybe wiggle your toes a bit. Feel the ground beneath you, like you're plugging into the here and now.

3. Upward Bound: Slowly, shift your focus up through your knees, hips, and your tummy. Imagine your energy rising with each step.

4. Heart-Centered: The heart is where the action's at. Give it a sec of your attention. You can even put your hand there if you're feeling it.

5. Inhale Confidence: Take a nice, deep breath in, and quietly tell yourself "I am." Feel your confidence growing with every breath.

6. Hold and Believe: Hold your breath briefly, and then say another "I am." Believe in your awesome self.

7. Exhale Power: Breathe out slooowly and drop another "I am." Release any stress or doubts, and soak up the self-belief.

8. Repeat, if You Dig: If you've got a bit more time, loop through this cycle 3-5 times. It's like a self-boosting mantra!

9. Give Your Soul a High-Five: Flash a teeny smile at yourself. You just had a quick soul-chat!

10. Peep Those Peepers: When you're good to go, open your eyes (if you closed them) and hop back into your day. You've just powered up with some self-awareness and swagger.

CHAPTER 2

BRIDGING THE GENERATION GAP

Have you ever felt like adults can be a bit puzzling? It's not that we want to question your parents' wisdom; they're doing their best, just like all parents. Sometimes, though, they might be so accustomed to seeing you as their little one, always needing guidance and decisions made for you, that they forget to acknowledge the growing, capable individual you're becoming. It's as if they've been so used to caring for you that they occasionally overlook your budding independence. It's not on purpose; it's just because parents are learning and adapting along with you. In other words, they're still figuring this whole parenting thing out as you grow up.

Remember, being a teenager is like having one foot in childhood and the other in adulthood. It's a time of change, self-discovery, and exploring the world around you. So, if you ever feel misunderstood or like you're constantly navigating a maze of expectations, just know that it's a shared experience for many teens. Your parents are doing their best to guide you, but they're also learning to let you spread your wings and make your own choices.

Imagine, from the moment you were born, you embarked on a remarkable journey of learning how to be human. You took your very first steps, uttered your first words, discovered the magic of reading, and reveled in the joy of playtime. It was like you had an empty canvas for a mind, and with every passing day, you filled it with knowledge and experiences. You didn't come into this world knowing what it meant to be someone's child; instead, you learned it step by step.

But here's the fascinating part: just as you were learning to navigate the world, your parents were on their own learning journey, too. Even if you have older siblings, it doesn't automatically make your parents experts in parenting. They embarked on this adventure of parenthood when you entered their lives, and they've been figuring it out along the way.

You see, your parents, despite their love and care for you, are human beings with their own set of fears, doubts, and uncertainties. They have the same everyday worries as anyone else. They worry about making the right decisions, guiding you in the best way possible, and ensuring your happiness and safety. Sometimes, they might even feel like they're walking in the dark, trying to find the right path, just like you do in life.

So, remember, being a teenager is not just about your own growth and self-discovery; it's also about understanding that your parents are growing and learning right alongside you. It's a journey you're all taking together, filled with ups and downs, lessons learned, and love that keeps growing stronger.

Imagine you're a bridge, a bridge between generations. On one side, there's your parents with all their experiences, hopes, and dreams. On the other side, there's you, with your unique perspective on the world. It's your job to connect these two worlds, to help your parents see things from your point of view, and to understand that you're growing into an independent individual.

It won't always be easy, and there might be moments when you feel like they're not listening or don't understand. But don't give up. Keep the lines of communication open. Share your thoughts and feelings with them, even if they don't always agree. Remember, it's a two-way bridge, you also need to be willing to listen and understand their perspective.

By helping your parents see you as a person with your own thoughts and feelings, you'll be paving the way for a stronger and more respectful relationship. And who knows, maybe together, you can break free from those old patterns and create a brighter future for yourselves as a family. It's all part of growing up and learning together, as you become more independent and your parents learn to support and trust you in making your own decisions.

Practice:

Now, let's delve into another practice that can help bridge the gap between you and your parents.

1. Find a quiet and peaceful place for yourself, and if you'd like, play some soothing music to create a peaceful atmosphere. Ask that no one disturb you during this time. It's your special moment for reflection and growth.

2. Think back to a recent disagreement or dissatisfaction you had with one of your parents. What did they say or do that made you feel angry, upset, or annoyed? Bring that situation to the forefront of your mind.

3. Now, here's where it gets interesting. Imagine,

just in your thoughts, that you're stepping into your parent's shoes. Try to feel what your parent might have felt during that conversation. Picture the situation from their perspective. What thoughts and emotions could have been swirling in their minds? How might they have been feeling at that very moment?

4. As you take on your parent's point of view, think about what they might wish to change about themselves in that situation. Then, consider what you, as their child, could do differently to make things better.

5. Now, let's try a different perspective. Imagine your parent looking at you with understanding, kindness, and deep love. Picture yourself as your parent sees you: their beloved child. Forget about any dissatisfaction or worries for now. Just focus on being loved for who you are. No more, no less.

6. Next, we'll switch it up again. This is quite interesting too. Imagine looking at your parents

from the outside, as if they were the same age as you. Try to imagine how they might have felt during that conversation. What thoughts and emotions might be going through their minds? What could they be feeling at that very moment?

7. As you take on this different perspective, think about what your parent, as a fellow teenager, might want to change about themselves in this situation. Then, consider what you, as a teenager, could have done differently to improve things. Really get into this fresh way of looking at things.

8. After you finish this exercise, take some time to sit down and write down all the thoughts and ideas that came to you. What did you learn about yourself and your relationship with your parent? How can this new way of thinking help you connect better with them?

Remember, this exercise isn't about placing blame or justifying actions. It's about building empathy, understanding, and gaining deeper insight into your relationships. By doing this, you can create bridges of love and open communication, making your family bonds even stronger.

CHAPTER 3

THE MAGIC OF MINDSET

Imagine a world filled with settings, much like the settings on your favourite video game or the options on your smartphone. You might be wondering, "What are these settings, and why are they important?" Let's dive into this fascinating concept.

Every day, we encounter countless messages about life, happiness, and who we are. Books, intriguing people, TV shows, and social media are constantly bombarding us with ideas and phrases, but few truly explain how this all works. It's time to unravel the mystery.

Consider this: Our bodies are made up of about 50-70% water, and similarly, our minds are composed of about 50-70% of what we think about. In simple terms, what we think, feel, and believe shapes our reality. If we nurture negative thoughts and beliefs, they can become our dominant settings, radiating out into the world.

For example, if someone convinces themselves that nobody finds them interesting, a remarkable transformation takes place. They start to project an aura of disinterest, and it becomes a self-fulfilling prophecy. The tricky thing about these settings is that sometimes they seem to operate beyond our control.

Picture this: A girl tells a boy that his teeth are unattractive, and his smile repulses people. What happens next? The boy takes her words to heart and starts believing that his smile is indeed repulsive. Consequently, when he smiles, people react negatively. But here's the catch: he unknowingly created this reality himself.

The wonderful thing is that we have the power to change our settings. Just like in a video game where you can adjust the difficulty level, you can tweak your mindset. As children grow into adults, these childhood attitudes evolve, but here's the good news: you can take charge of them.

Imagine that boy challenging the girl's opinion and saying, "That's just your perspective, and it doesn't align with mine." Suddenly, his smile shines radiantly, and nobody notices his crooked tooth anymore. It's as if he's switched to a new, more positive setting.

In life, there are no real miracles, but there's something equally magical: the power of your mindset. By choosing to believe in yourself and your own worth, you can transform your reality. Your life can be filled with radiant smiles, positivity, and an unwavering belief in your unique charm.

So, my young adventurer, remember this: You have the incredible ability to set your own course in life by adjusting the settings of your mind. Choose wisely, believe in your brilliance, and watch the world around you light up with the magic of your mindset.

Practice:

Now that we've uncovered the importance of our mental settings, it's time to put our detective hats on and embark on a transformative practice. You see, deep within our minds, there are attitudes and beliefs that often remain hidden, affecting our outlook on life. Let's shine a light on them and turn them into sources of positivity.

For this exercise, you'll need a notepad and two pens of different colours. Throughout the day, whenever you catch yourself thinking a negative thought, jot it down in your notepad. It's like collecting evidence as a detective would in a case.

At the end of the day, when you have a moment of peace and quiet, sit down with your notepad. Take a look at all those negative thoughts you've gathered. Now, it's time to work your magic. Transform these negative attitudes into positive ones.

Here's how it works: Take a pen of a different colour and cross out the negative thought. Then, right beside it, rewrite the thought in a positive light (you can use the extra space at the back of the book if you don't have journal available). Let me give you a few examples to illustrate:

1. *Negative Thought:* "I have no friends at all, and this boy/girl won't be friends with me either."

Positive Transformation: "I have many good and loyal friends, and I'm open to making new friends."

2. *Negative Thought:* "I will never save up for this thing (insert what you dream about here)."

Positive Transformation: "I am taking steps to save up for the things I dream about, and I can achieve my goals."

3. *Negative Thought:* "Nobody listens to me, so I won't even try to tell you anything."

Positive Transformation: "I am an interesting storyteller, and I have important things to share. People value what I say."

Discovering and changing negative attitudes can be a bit like a game. It's not just about crossing them out in different colors on a piece of paper; you'll need to work on changing them every day. Sometimes, a specific attitude might stick with you, feeling pretty comfortable. But guess what? It's actually pretty easy to change this. Since you might not always have a notepad and pencil on hand, try these steps during the day:

1. First, notice when you're having a negative attitude.

2. Imagine it like a phrase floating in the air.

3. In your mind, cross out that phrase with your favorite color.

4. Let it disappear into the air.

5. Finally, give it a smile.

Take a few deep breaths, and quietly say to yourself, "I am." Feel the love within you. After all, that attitude was once a part of you, and like you, it deserves some love. So, smile at it and transform it with love.

As you keep doing this, it'll help you think more

positively and feel better about life. Just remember, you're in charge of your own story, and this exercise is like a superpower that helps you do that. But there's more to it; it's not just your big thoughts that influence your mindset. Your everyday experiences play a part too, and that's what we'll explore next.

I want to share with you the idea that every person is incredibly unique and one-of-a-kind. We each possess a multitude of different qualities, and it's crucial to recognize that what others may perceive as negative isn't necessarily a true reflection of who we are. Our inner beauty and self-confidence should be rooted in our own beliefs and not solely influenced by those around us.

Think of it this way: Just like in Chapter 2 when we put ourselves in our parents' shoes to see situations from different angles, here, we're examining the concept of perspective. For instance, let's say you didn't want to share your last apple with someone, and they labeled you as greedy. Are you truly greedy? Well, if you view it from their perspective, it might seem that way. But what if we look at it from your point of view?

Your body desired that crisp, juicy apple, and it happened to be your last one, so you made a choice to care for yourself by enjoying it. Looking at it this way, you were not being greedy; you were simply taking care of your own needs.

Now, let's explore another scenario: What if you desired to keep the apple for yourself, but instead, you gave it away out of fear that others might brand you as greedy? In this situation, you might not seem greedy in the eyes of others, but deep down, you know that you were greedy for yourself. This act of self-denial was driven solely by the desire to gain their approval.

I understand that the apple example may seem quite straightforward and illustrative, but I used it to help you grasp the concept. Finding positivity within what may seem negative is an art that, like our previous exercises, requires practice to reshape our thinking patterns.

Absolutely crucial to grasp is that you should never try to justify your wrongdoings. Yet, it's even more critical to understand why you might have done something that others didn't appreciate but could have been beneficial to you. You must master the art of viewing the same situation from various perspectives. It's about recognizing when it's the right time to be your own ally and when it's an opportunity to assist others.

Our individuality wasn't bestowed upon us without purpose; it was given to us so we could share it with the world. However, to begin sharing your uniqueness, you must first learn to listen to yourself, stand by yourself, and embrace yourself. The moment you start embracing yourself just as you are, you'll also embrace everyone else for their unique selves.

Practice: Exploring Different Angles

Now, let's dive into a practice that will help you understand the importance of seeing things from various perspectives.

1. Find a comfortable and quiet space where you won't be disturbed. Sit down, close your eyes, and take a few deep breaths to relax.

2. Think about a recent situation where you did something that someone didn't like or approve of, but you felt it was necessary or beneficial for you.

3. Visualize that situation in your mind. Try to recall as many details as possible, including what you did and how others reacted.

4. Now, imagine you're viewing the same situation from the perspective of the person who didn't like your actions. What might they have been thinking and feeling? How did your actions

appear from their point of view?

5.   Next, switch your perspective. See the situation through your own eyes, but this time, try to understand why you made that choice. What were your thoughts and emotions at that moment? What benefit or necessity did you see in your actions?

Reflect on what you've learned from this exercise. Did it help you gain insight into the situation? Did it make you realize that sometimes, doing what's right for you may not align with others' opinions?

Write down your reflections in a journal or notebook. Consider how you can use this newfound understanding to make better choices in the future, both for yourself and in your interactions with others.

Remember, this exercise isn't about saying your actions were right when they were wrong. It's more about understanding how different people see things. It's like having a special skill that helps you figure out life's tricky parts and appreciate what makes you special.

CHAPTER 4

THE POWER OF EARLY SLEEP

Sleep, my dear friend, is a remarkable and essential process that recharges and restores our bodies. It's like a supercharger for your mind and body, and it's especially crucial for you, the young adventurer. Let's explore the science behind why going to bed early can be your secret weapon for energy, health, and boss-level thinking.

Why Should You Sleep Early?

1. Healing Time: Sleep is like a mini hospital for your body. After a long day of playing, learning, and running around, your body needs time to fix any tiny damages. When you sleep, your body gets busy fixing these damages, so you need a good amount of sleep to feel fresh and strong the next day.

2. Growth Juice: When you sleep, your body makes a special juice called growth hormone that helps you grow taller and stronger. If you don't get enough sleep, your body can't make enough of this growth juice.

3. Remembering Stuff: Sleep is like a trusted friend that helps you remember things better. When you learn something new, sleep acts as your memory's guardian, ensuring that your brain stores that information securely for later recall.

4. Happy Mood: If you sleep well, you wake up feeling happy and relaxed. But if you don't sleep enough, you might feel grumpy or sad. Sleep is like a happy pill that keeps your mood nice and cheerful.

5. Staying Healthy: If you keep missing out on sleep, over time, it can make you sick. It's like your body's shield against illnesses gets weaker. So, sleeping well keeps your shield strong and keeps you healthy.

6. Dream Time: There's a special part of sleep called REM sleep, when you have dreams. This part is super important for feeling rested. Youngsters have their REM sleep a bit later in the night, so sleeping early makes sure you get enough dream time.

7. Ready for Learning: Learning starts early, right? If you stay up late, you won't get enough sleep, and you might feel too sleepy when it's time to learn. Sleeping early helps you wake up on time, feeling fresh and ready to learn new things!

A Nighttime Ritual for Blissful Sleep:

Now, let's talk about creating a nighttime ritual that will set the stage for a restful slumber. Here's your bedtime checklist:

1. Ventilation: Ensure your sleep space has fresh air. Open the window and draw the curtains. This simple step can enhance your sleep quality.

2. Food Curfew: Stop eating at least an hour before bedtime. Give your body the luxury of resting at night instead of digesting food.

3. Screen-Free Zone: Say goodbye to your phone and other screens an hour before bed. Your brain might whisper, "Just one more message or video won't hurt," but give your mind the luxury of true rest. Instead, read a book, draw, or write in a journal—engage in activities you've been meaning to do but kept postponing.

4. Bedtime Deadline: Make a promise to yourself to be in bed, ideally by 20:45 (I know, it might sound a bit early, but hang on!). This isn't just about sleeping, it's also your special time. You can read, think, plan for tomorrow, or even try some of the cool practices I share in this book. And guess what? You can give yourself a bit more time on weekends to enjoy those activities. It's a special treat you're giving to your body and mind to rest and recharge for all the adventures ahead!

5. Mindful Relaxation: As you lie down, focus on your breathing. Inhale and exhale, directing your breath through different parts of your body. Imagine tension leaving your legs, then your stomach, your chest, and finally your head. Relax your breath and peacefully drift into sleep or revisit the practice from Chapter 1.

I understand, most of your buddies are probably staying up late, scrolling through their phones or tablets – it's like a trend, right? And hey, I totally get that you might roll your eyes at my sleep advice. I mean, who hasn't thought, "Tonight, I'll stay up just a little later, and tomorrow, I'll totally wake up on time, no problem!" It's like a promise we make to ourselves every morning. But here's the deal, it's a bit of a trick we play on ourselves because when the evening rolls around, suddenly, sleep seems like the last thing we want. There's this urge to stay up and do anything but sleep.

Now, let me drop some wisdom on you – ditching

those gadgets in the evening and hitting the sack early? That's the new cool. Seriously, if you do some digging, you'll find that loads of famous and successful folks prefer the early-to-bed, early-to-rise routine. So, if one of your pals tries to argue the late-night case, you don't even have to debate. In fact, you can keep this whole sleep secret to yourself. Your friends will notice the change over time – you'll be on top of things, and they'll be curious about your secret. And when they ask, you can spill the beans without hesitation.

Here's the real deal: you're not missing out on anything by spending your evenings without gadgets and hitting the sack early. In fact, it's like you're leveling up. You'll wake up feeling refreshed, get to know yourself through some of the cool practices in this book, and give yourself that boost to a whole new level of awesomeness. So, let's get you on the path to supercharging your life!!

CHAPTER 5

THE JOY OF PHYSICAL ACTIVITY

Now that we've explored the magic of a good night's sleep, it's time to unlock another secret to a healthy and vibrant life: physical exercise. Whether you're not a sports enthusiast or someone who hasn't quite found the right activity yet, there's a world of physical activity waiting for you to discover.

Finding Your Passion in Sports

Firstly, let's talk about discovering a sport that truly ignites your passion. You see, there's a sport out there for everyone; you just need to find it. Fortunately, the world today offers a plethora of opportunities to explore different activities. Many clubs offer the chance to try your first lesson for free, be it karate, boxing, ballet, dancing (yes, dance is a sport too), yoga, various martial arts, and so much more. If you can't find something nearby, consider asking the adults in your life to help you find age-appropriate video activities online. In our digital age, the internet is a treasure trove of possibilities. Try, discard what doesn't resonate with you, and keep searching for what you genuinely enjoy. Listen to yourself – we'll delve into this later.

Morning Warm-Up: Fuelling Your Day

However, I'd like to introduce an equally excellent option, especially for those of you who might not have access to clubs or prefer to exercise at home. Later, we'll discuss the significance of mornings in shaping our day. Think of your body as a plant; like a plant stretches toward the sun in the morning, physical activity helps your body reach its full potential. When you move in the morning, you help your body wake up, prepare your mind to think clearly, and fill yourself with energy for the day ahead. This keeps you cheerful, attentive, and ready for the adventures that await!

If you have the opportunity to step outside into the garden for your morning routine, that's wonderful. But if not, an open window will do just fine. I suggest selecting 2-3 exercises to choose from and spending 10 to 20 minutes as desired.

Here are some ideas to get you started:

1. Jumping in Place: A simple yet effective way to get your blood flowing.

2. Push-Ups: Great for building upper body strength.

3. Squats: Excellent for strengthening your legs and core.

4. Plank: A core-strengthening exercise that also improves posture.

5. Flexibility Exercises: Stretching, bending, and bowing to keep your body limber.

6. Cardio Activities: Try jogging, skipping rope, or cycling to get your heart pumping.

7. Pull-Ups: If you have access to a pull-up bar, this exercise works wonders for your back and arm muscles.

It's crucial to have adults check your exercise form to ensure they're beneficial and safe. Proper execution is key to reaping the full benefits without risking injury.

The Fun and Importance of Staying Active

Ever wondered why we bother with physical exercise beyond the whole 'staying in shape' thing? Well, here's the deal: Exercise isn't just about looking great; it's about living great. Let me break it down for you.

When we get up and get active, whether it's playing sports, going for a jog, or even just a brisk walk, something pretty amazing goes on inside our bodies. It's like a rush of energy surging through us, like a rollercoaster ride for our insides—up, down, and all around. It's an explosion of excitement and power coursing through our veins. But here's the twist: if we don't tap into this energy through physical exercise, it just kinda sits there, twiddling its thumbs. And you know what happens when something sits around doing nothing, right? Not much of anything exciting!

Now, let's chat about a cool practice, especially handy when you can't do the usual exercises for some reason – it's the 'Walking Practice.' It's as simple as pie, and you can slip it into your routine anytime you're on the move.

31

Walking Practice:

Alright, here's the scoop: Whether you're heading out to study, going to the store, or running small chores, try to walk with a little extra pep in your step. Imagine each walk as a mini adventure. Feel how every part of your body joins in on the fun!

How can you make this adventure exciting? It's easy! Just pay extra attention to how you walk. Feel how your feet hit the ground, how your arms swing back and forth, and how your breath goes in and out. It's like tuning into a secret channel where you can feel the energy dancing in your body.

And at the end of this chapter, I will give you a very special exercise: Imagine there's a tiny ball of energy in your feet. When you breathe in, picture this energy ball traveling up to the top of your head. And when you breathe out, see it traveling back down to your feet. Try doing this a few times, like 2 or 3 times, whenever you can during the day. You can do this while standing near a window, looking out at the world. Each time you do this, you wake up the sleeping energy inside you. If you want to do this energy exercise more times, go ahead! It's a fun way to feel more alive and ready for anything. So, give it a try and see how it makes your day a bit more exciting!

CHAPTER 6

CREATING A CHAIN OF POSITIVITY

Have you ever thought about how one little thing can lead to another? Like, imagine waking up feeling grumpy, then you accidentally argue with someone, forget to grab something important, bump into a not-so-happy person on your way, and find yourself in another argument later on. It's like a domino effect of not-so-great stuff. But, what if we flip the script? You wake up to birds chirping, a smile blossoms on your face, the yummy smell of your favourite breakfast floats in, and you head out feeling calm. Along the way, someone shares a friendly smile with you, and your day keeps getting brighter. It's a domino effect again, but of good vibes this time. One happy moment leads to another, and another. It all boils down to where you let your attention zoom. Your attention is like a flashlight, whatever it shines on, gets lit up with your energy.

Here's a neat little trick to kickstart a chain of happy moments:

Before you snuggle into bed at night, think about one small thing you're looking forward to the next day. It could be anything - a tasty breakfast, hanging out with a friend, or even a day off. Lock that thought in your mind, and let it be the first thing that pops up when you wake up. Smile when you remember it. Your happy chain has just begun! As your day rolls on, keep an eye out for more happy moments. It's like collecting gems of joy. Every happy moment you spot is like adding a bead to your bracelet of good vibes.

Now, let's talk about something pretty important – being kind to those around you. Think of kindness as these little bursts of positivity you throw into the world. When you do that, it's like you're adding a splash of color and cheerfulness to everything around you. The interesting part is that how you treat others often finds its way back to you, just like a boomerang. So, when you send out good vibes by being kind, helpful, and understanding, you'll discover those good vibes bouncing back to you in the most unexpected and delightful ways.

Make it a goal to be the kind of person you'd genuinely enjoy meeting. Whether it's sharing a friendly smile, offering a hand, or simply being there for someone, every sprinkle of kindness you spread adds to your chain of happy moments and brightens up the world a little more. Being kind isn't just about making others feel good; it's like planting little seeds of joy that eventually grow into a garden of positivity around you. And guess what? You get to enjoy the beauty of that garden because you planted those seeds of kindness!

By the end of this chapter, I hope it's crystal clear to you that the person you should be the kindest to is none other than yourself. When you speak kindly to yourself, acknowledge your achievements, and find joy in everything you have, you're setting off a remarkable chain reaction of positive events all around you.

But life isn't always a walk in the park, and that's perfectly fine. There will be moments when things don't go as planned, and it's okay to feel a little miffed or frustrated. Bottling up those feelings isn't the answer, though. Instead, try this: pause for a moment and take a deep breath. Imagine yourself riding gentle waves on a calm sea as you inhale and exhale. Let a sense of calmness wrap around you like a warm, comfy blanket. In these quiet moments, you might just discover a silver lining in those cloudy situations, something to learn or a humorous side to it all.

But, here's the twist – don't approach this with the idea of forcing positive thoughts. Positive thinking is like playing a role; it's pretending. In reality, it's perfectly normal to grapple with various emotions, even the not-so-great ones. Acknowledging them is crucial. Recognize these feelings, accept them as part of who you are, and remember that it's entirely okay to experience emotions like anger, frustration, irritation, sadness, or even despondency. The key is to shift your focus toward the good things, and you'll find more of them surrounding you.

So, my fellow young adventurer, always remember this: You possess the incredible ability to chart your own course in life by adjusting the settings of your mind. Choose wisely, believe in your brilliance, and watch as the world around you lights up with the magic of your mindset.

Let's wrap it up:

Step 1: The Nighttime Spark

Before you snuggle into bed tonight, take a moment to think about one small thing you're looking forward to the next day. It could be a delicious breakfast, a chat with a friend, or simply having some free time. Imagine it vividly, and let it settle in your mind as you drift off to sleep.

Step 2: Morning Sunshine

As you wake up, allow that positive thought from the previous night to be the first thing on your mind. Feel it. Smile at it. Let this small moment of anticipation set a positive tone for your day.

Step 3: Gem Collection

Throughout your day, keep an eye out for moments that bring a smile to your face, no matter how small they seem. It could be a friendly gesture, a funny sight, or a moment of tranquility. Collect these "gems of joy" mentally, like adding beads to your bracelet.

Step 4: Spread Kindness

In your day, try to be kind to others. Smile, help, or be there when someone needs you. See how this positivity affects your mood and interactions.

Step 5: Reflect and Share

At the end of the day, take a moment to reflect on the positive moments and the kindness you've shared. Consider how they influenced your day. If you feel comfortable, share your experiences with someone close to you or even in a journal.

Step 6: Embrace Feelings

It's okay to have tough moments in your day. When negative thoughts or feelings arise, accept them. Take deep breaths, let them pass like clouds in the sky. This process strengthens your journey toward a positive mindset.

CHAPTER 7

TUNING INTO THE WHISPERS OF YOUR SOUL

We're diving into something super important now: how to hear yourself, make big decisions, and figure out what you really want. Think of it as having a built-in truth detector or a personal compass – let's call it your soul. I know it might sound a bit mysterious, but trust me, it's not hocus-pocus; it's something inside all of us.

Have you ever had a feeling that you just shouldn't do something, even if you couldn't explain why? Or perhaps, you felt an irresistible pull toward doing something that filled you with excitement and joy. In those moments, you were actually hearing your soul. But here's the thing: your soul doesn't talk with words; it communicates through feelings. Sometimes it makes you feel calm and comfy, like a cozy blanket, when something is right for you. Other times, it gives you a strong "NO" feeling, like a loud alarm going off inside you when something doesn't align with your true self.

Now, here's the cool part: by practicing, you can get better at listening to your soul. And when you're facing important decisions, that skill can be super handy. Start small, and little by little, you'll learn to hear your soul's wisdom whenever you need it most.

So, let's get practicing:

1. Soul Whispers: Find a quiet spot where you won't be disturbed. Close your eyes, take a deep breath, and let it out slowly. Imagine you're in a calm and peaceful place – it could be a sunny beach, a quiet forest, or anywhere that feels good to you. Now, think about a small decision you need to make, like what book to read or what game to play. Pay attention to how your body feels when you think about each option. Does one choice make you feel lighter and happier, while the other feels heavy or anxious? Trust those feelings – that's your soul talking to you. Go with the choice that feels right, and notice how it turns out. As you practice this with small decisions, you're like a detective learning to trust the clues your feelings provide. You're not just deciding on small things; you're training yourself to understand your inner guidance. With each tiny choice, you get to know your 'soul whispers' better. It's similar to learning a new language - the language of your intuition. Over time, as you get more comfortable and skilled in understanding these whispers, you'll find it easier to make bigger decisions. Whether it's choosing a hobby, deciding on a project, or even standing up for a friend, you'll have a growing trust in this inner voice. It's a gentle journey from picking a book to read, to making choices that shape your adventures. Each step, no matter how small, is a leap towards becoming more in tune with yourself. So, start with the small stuff and watch how your soul guides you towards bigger, exciting choices as you grow. It's like having a wise friend inside you, helping you along the way! Remember, your soul doesn't talk with words; it uses your feelings. Instead of following your mind, focus on creating your own path.

2. Soul Journal: Get a notebook or a piece of paper, and at the end of each day, write down one thing that brought you joy and one thing that offered a valuable lesson. It could be as simple as enjoying your lunch or learning from a challenging moment with a friend. Then, jot down how your body felt in those moments – did you feel relaxed or tense, happy or thoughtful? Over time, you'll start to notice patterns. You'll see what situations and choices align with your inner sense of happiness and what provides opportunities for growth. This journal will become your trusty guide in making decisions that truly resonate with your deepest self.

3. Wishful Thinking: Take a moment to think about something you really wish for – it could be a new toy, a fun adventure, or spending time with a friend. Picture it vividly in your mind. Now, ask yourself: Is this wish coming from my heart, or is it something I think I should want because someone else does or because it's popular? Your soul knows your true desires. If the wish feels genuine, like a warm, glowing spark inside you, that's your soul telling you it's something you truly want. But if it feels like a distant star, far away and not quite yours, it might be a wish that doesn't align with your deepest self. Trust your soul's guidance to help you discover your real wishes, those that bring you genuine happiness and fulfilment. Over time, you'll become more attuned to your heart's true desires and make choices that lead to greater joy and contentment.

Alright, so imagine you have a smart buddy right inside you, always ready to help you out! This buddy talks to you through feelings, like when something feels good or not so good. Every day, as you get better at listening to this buddy, making choices becomes easier and more fun. So, whenever you're not sure what to do, take a moment to listen to this inner buddy. You need always remember that it's similar to having a supportive friend accompanying you on this exciting journey of life, constantly there to assist you along the way!

SUMMARY

Hey there, awesome reader! We've wrapped up this book, and it's been quite a journey, right? Let's do a quick recap to make sure we're all on the same wavelength about what this book is all about.

Chapter 1: The Importance of Self-Love

In this chapter, we dived into the wonderful world of self-love. We learned that self-love is like giving yourself a warm hug, not being selfish. It's about treating yourself with kindness and understanding that you're a superstar in your own life. We even tried out a self-love meditation to water the garden of self-love within you. Remember, a little self-love goes a long way!

Chapter 2: Bridging the Generation Gap

This chapter was all about the parent-teen relationship rollercoaster. We discovered that we're like bridges between generations, helping communication flow smoothly with our parents. We practiced putting ourselves in their shoes, building empathy, and strengthening the bonds with our family. It's all about teamwork on this crazy journey of life!

Chapter 3: The Magic of Mindset

Mindset, oh yeah! This chapter showed us the incredible power of our thoughts. Your mindset is like the remote control for your life, shaping your reality. We learned that we can change negative thoughts into positive ones and that empathy is like a superpower that helps us understand ourselves and others better.

Chapter 4: The Power of Early Sleep

Alright, sleep might not sound super exciting, but it's a total game-changer! Getting enough Zzzs is like fuel for your body and mind. We talked about the magic of going to bed early and how it sets you up for success. And guess what? We shared a cool bedtime routine to help you get the best sleep ever!

Chapter 5: The Joy of Physical Activity

Now, let's get moving! This chapter was all about the fun and awesomeness of physical exercise. We encouraged you to explore different activities, find your passion, and even gave you a morning warm-up routine to kickstart your day with energy and enthusiasm. Remember, exercise isn't just about looking good; it's about feeling great!

Chapter 6: Creating a Chain of Positivity

Positivity is like a magical chain reaction, and we dived into it in this chapter. You learned that positive thoughts and actions can light up your day and make the world a happier place. We talked about the power of kindness, not just for others but also for yourself. And hey, embracing your feelings is totally cool too. It's all about finding the silver lining in life's twists and turns.

Chapter 7: Tuning into the Whispers of Your Soul

Last but not least, we explored the whispers of your soul. Your inner self is like your personal compass, guiding you through life's adventures. We practiced listening to those feelings and understanding what your heart truly desires. It's like having a wise friend inside you, helping you make awesome choices.

So, there you have it – a quick recap of this fantastic journey we've been on. Remember, you have the power to shape your life, be kind, and listen to your inner wisdom. You're the star of your own show, and the world is your playground. Keep rocking, awesome reader!.

Personal Journal Of Your Inner Self

Personal Journal Of Your Inner Self

Personal Journal Of Your Inner Self

Personal Journal Of Your Inner Self

Personal Journal Of Your Inner Self

Personal Journal Of Your Inner Self

Personal Journal Of Your Inner Self

20:45: Unlocking Your Inner Magic

Personal Journal Of Your Inner Self

Personal Journal Of Your Inner Self

Personal Journal Of Your Inner Self

Personal Journal Of Your Inner Self

Personal Journal Of Your Inner Self

Personal Journal Of Your Inner Self

20:45: Unlocking Your Inner Magic

Personal Journal Of Your Inner Self

Personal Journal Of Your Inner Self

Personal Journal Of Your Inner Self

Personal Journal Of Your Inner Self

Personal Journal Of Your Inner Self

Personal Journal Of Your Inner Self

Personal Journal Of Your Inner Self

ABOUT THE AUTHOR

Stasia Smith is a London-based writer who is no stranger
to the whirlwind of adolescence. Raising three kids herself,
she understands the challenges and joys of growing up.
Stasia's approach is uniquely creative and deeply soulful,
drawing from her own memories of those confusing
teenage years. Her writing is filled with relatable insights
and practical guidance, making it an invaluable resource for
teenagers on their journey of self-discovery and self-love.

Printed in Great Britain
by Amazon

33967530R00044